Scanning the Horizon

Mark Miller

Scanning the Horizon

Dedicated to my mother
Joan Mary Miller
1920–2011

Scanning the Horizon
ISBN 978 1 76041 637 9
Copyright © text Mark Miller 2018
Cover: Lloyd Rees (Australia, b. 1895, d. 1988), *The Road to Berry*,
1947, oil on canvas on paperboard, 34.6 x 42.2 cm,
Art Gallery of New South Wales, purchased 1947,
© Estate of Lloyd Rees, Photo AGNSW, 7940

First published 2018 by
GINNINDERRA PRESS
PO Box 3461 Port Adelaide 5015 Australia
www.ginninderrapress.com.au

Contents

Approachings	7
This Estuary	9
Night Falls	10
Along Back Forest Road	11
Autumn, an Old Woman Remembers	12
For My Father	13
Approaching Winter	15
Somewhere in Central Australia	16
Flood-bound: Waiting	17
Incident on a Busy Back Road	18
Along the Red Dirt Road: Drought Country Sequence	20
Woman Crying in the Supermarket	24
Haven	25
Small Town, Saturday	26
Loss	27
Rabbiting	28
Night of Storm	29
The Ache of It	30
Variations on Rain in the Time of Drought	31
Haiku: Loss	33
Land's Edge, Winter	34
Ridge Fire, Morning Alight	36
What it is I Wanted to Say	37
Scanning the Horizon	39
Shoalhaven River, First Light	41
Bagatelles	43
Coastal Walk	44
T'ai Chi in the Park	48
Mix of Things	49

Eight Haiku	50
By the Estuary	51
Closing Time	55
Returning Home	56
On Contemplating *Cold Crow, Withered Tree* (1680)	57
Hiking up Bugong Creek	58
Six Vignettes of the Shoalhaven	59
Cow Escaped in the Night	61
The Return	62
From the Headland	65
Scanning the Horizon	66
On Finding a Pair of Shoes on the Beach	68
Postcards from the Coast	69
Haiku Sequence: In the Zen Garden	73
Notes	74
Acknowledgements	75
A note on the author	78

Approachings

This Estuary

This morning the mist
comes apart before me,
like fabric, like ashes –

revealing at low tide
the craters in sand
left by night-anglers
pumping for bait

sea-wrack and bottle-caps,
necklaces of purple sea-grapes,
bluebottles and ribboned weed

and like part of an old
bicycle tyre twisted
a bludgeoned eel,
its hooked mouth
hauled into a snarl –

this estuary,
opaque sheet of glass,
grey water under a greyer sky.

Night Falls

Night falls for the mushrooms
plush and belly-up in the fecund air.

It falls for the dairyman
stamping his steaming boots at the farmhouse door,
for the black boardriders flensing back flaps of the glistening water.

It falls for the whooping girls on the hockey field,
for the magpie weaving its lofty nest.

It falls for the morning jogger
exhaling the vapour of his smouldering pain,
for the panic-stricken rabbit escaping on the rim of shadow.

It falls for the cars gridlocked on the highway,
for the woman cradling the steaming cup
in her knotted hands.

Night falls for the broken man in the prison yard,
for the factory workers unbuckling their leather aprons.

It falls for the lovers in their evening dress,
for the doctor, the publican, the engineer, the poet,

for the neighbour's dog at the gate
waiting for its master.

Along Back Forest Road

Cycling along
Back Forest Road
just over a crest
on a hot afternoon
we came upon him –
a red-bellied black
caught by careless tyres
half on bitumen
and half in the stony shoulder.
The black lurex
along his back
to his cold, opaque glare
splashed silver at our eyes,
a fly buzzed
where a red-crimson droplet
had dried near his tiny head.
We marvelled
at his own carelessness –
curved and silent like the road,
drugged in the fatal heat –
and we pedalled on,
certain that day
we'd not seen anything living
half as splendid
as this death
on our long ride home.

Autumn, an Old Woman Remembers

It always begins with smells –

the vaporised frost at dawn
infused with mulched leaves of the garden

the scent of eucalyptus
under pungent drops of an afternoon squall

the chimney smoke thick with pine,
and weighed down with evening's dew –

it always begins with smells –
the mustiness of a shut room

the staleness of potpourri in the upper
corner of the dresser drawer

the photo album clumsily disturbed,
the images evoking

the taffeta smell of the christening gown,
the milk dribble of the infant in a woman's arms

the priest's incense and tobacco-steeped garments,
the earthiness of the raw clay mound

on the cemetery's bitten lawn.

For My Father

1 Saturdays Home From Boarding School

Even on Saturdays my father would rise early,
in the cold-bleak and crackling dawn,
well before I heard him in the kitchen,
stoking the fire and making fried bread –
never French toast – from the leftover dripping
and stale bread he'd kept in the cupboard.

He would bring it to me on a tray –
such a delicious start to weekends away from school.
How could I not love him, how could
I not love this stranger, who made such offerings,
who would be gone before I got up

and would come home in the evenings too late,
too drunk, to see his newly polished work shoes,
his covered tea sitting on the cold stove-top plate,
and my finished homework, left open on the bench,
near where the lamplight stayed on.

2 Cleaning Out the Drawer

I find a photo of my father.
Nothing extraordinary, just standing
in his overalls in the doorway,
maybe returning from work
or coming back from feeding the chooks,
a cigarette dangling from the fingers of his left hand,
his hat at a tilt over the right brow,
and his angular body dully back-lit.

Our eyes meet across the threshold,
but what do I know about this man
now that he's gone from my life,
I who am now his age
and making all the mistakes
that I thought were his.

Approaching Winter

for my mother

I think of phoning you
in the milk-white of dawn
hundreds of kilometres away
where you are probably
lighting the electric heater –

>   *taking longer to get started –*

on your morning chores
making the strong tea
and taking a biscuit or two
with your tablets –

>   *nothing eases the pain –*

and not being bothered
to make breakfast –

>   *everything's a burden –*

you just want to go back to your bed
to your only comfort
the voices of radio –

>   *can't get around like before –*

you draw the curtains
grey clouds covering the mountain
threaten snow
before the day is out
before the phone call comes.

Somewhere in Central Australia

Rattling,
shaking through dust
in the old truck –

in the back
with empty petrol barrels
two Aborigines:

a young mother
and her daughter
crying

scratching the red
welts of her skin.

The truck shakes on,
the earth rumbles.

In the rear-vision mirror
the sky has strangely
clouded over –

The daughter wails.
I push down harder
on the pedal –

I am my father.

It is 1953.

Flood-bound: Waiting

From the homestead's veranda
I watch her under the sieved moonlight,
her skin silken and dully silver.

Incredibly, after three days she dozes
but does not sleep.

I could almost reach out,
run my fingers through her tresses,
listen to her runnelled sighs.

But she betrays such closeness:
just this morning, miles downstream,
they pulled from her grasp the muddy boot
of our neighbour's missing child.

Incident on a Busy Back Road

Just over the rise
I come upon them,
four figures kneeling by the roadside
as if in prayer
or peering into a well,
the bright primaries –
the yellows and reds of their clothing –
and the silver of their splayed bicycles
piercing the new light of morning.

Slowing to the opposite side,
I stop and wind down the window
and it's then I see between the passing cars
two women are taking turns
pumping the chest
of a prostrate man.
He moves under their thrusts
but lies still afterwards.
Anxiously, they look around,
a car and trailer have stopped behind them,
the alighting driver
already offering his mobile.
There are six there now,
with another driver stopping
and leaning over
the one who doesn't move…

I drive slowly from the edge,
merging into the traffic

as other cars stop on the opposite side.
There is nothing I or other drivers can do now
but drive on
to our own appointments,
in this brittle light of morning
the road sweeping blindly on.

Along the Red Dirt Road: Drought Country Sequence

1

Wildlife Crossing
pinpoints of light through
the bullet holes.

2

Heatwave
the horizon's haze
of locust nymphs.

3

Wedge-tailed eagles
the farmer counts
his lambs.

4

Gum-tree bark
the dreamtime art
of scribbly moths.

5

Drought
rising out of the dam water
the old disc plough.

6

Mid-stride
pausing to taste the wind
a dingo pup.

7

Raucous cockatoos
the farmer's gaze turns
to the horizon.

8

Ongoing drought
the stillness
of the rope swing.

9

Small-town bar
an old farmer yarns with a mate
who isn't there.

10

Fire ban
overhead a goshawk fans
the thermal currents.

11

Blood-red moon
all day across the valley
the wail of sirens.

12

Back road at dusk
seeing a kangaroo
in every shadow.

13

Lone tree
by the roadside
a plywood cross.

14

Homestead fence
splayed and bloodied
the wings of a wedge-tailed eagle.

15

Auctioneer's spiel
the farm widow's
furrowed brow.

16

Nightfall
a man throws roadkill
into the tray of a truck.

17

Foreclosure
hidden by the brim of his hat
the farmer's eyes.

18

Another drought year
along the red dirt road
another hearse.

Woman Crying in the Supermarket

There's a woman crying
in the frozen food aisle
of the supermarket,
her tears are turning to ice on her cheeks,
her feet are encased in a pool of frozen tears.
She has one hand clutching her trolley
somewhere between the frozen peas
and the ice cream compartments,
her other hand holds a mobile to her ear,
her mouth is slightly open.
People file past her, they look, stare,
they want her to move.
The aisle is slippery,
beginning to ice over with her frozen tears,
trolleys become stuck,
clogging the whole aisle,
even Security can't budge her.
Soon emergency workers arrive
with sharp tools and pressure hoses.
The ice is chipped and liquefied around her.
Lifted and placed in a trolley
like a tumbled statue
she is pushed through the fractured ice
away from the aisle,
past the fresh food section
where a man holding a ticket
and wearing a fish on his head
waits impatiently
for the deli to reopen.

Haven

'because sometimes
walking
is all you know' (Peter Bakowski)

Five o'clock
on this pewter morning,
I take the winding track
through the thickets
of tea-tree and acacia,
in the distance
is the constant susurrus
of the high sea
tormented by wind.
Here, not even the grasping vines
and clawing branches,
or the honeyeaters and finches
with their needle calls piercing
the brittle skin of dawn
disturb my walking –
here, nothing else matters
but the sound
of my own breathing,
and my footsteps
taking me onwards.

Small Town, Saturday

It's afternoon
in high summer

hotel doors gape
at the baking street

mizzling flies
crawl over drinkers

race calls blare
through the open windows

a dog sleeps fitfully
in the veranda shade

a young woman,
captive of her dreams

waits upstairs
for the perfect stranger.

Loss

1

Grief pushes back the curtains,
rises from crumpled sheets
into the bathroom mirror,
staring back with its stolen face
of grief, and moves unsteadily
to the kitchen. Grief reaches
into the cupboard for tablets
and a cup, holding them
in trembling hands
before the glare of the window.
Grief washes. Grief dresses.
Grief silently steps outside
into the wish-parade of other faces,
into the stinging daylight wearing
the sun's wardrobe
of a thousand kitchen knives.

2

Leaving the Family Court –
the birds screaming
my own rage.

3

Her gloves
still
in my sock drawer.

Rabbiting

Dad and Uncle Brian would put nets
over burrows near logs and straggly bushes

they'd fetch and carry cages
from the tray of the old battered Ford
and let the ferrets run free down the mother holes

and while dad rolled a smoke
we'd wait and watch
until all hell would break loose
as rabbits and ferrets hurtled into the nets –

we'd do this for other burrows
each time recapturing the ferrets
and tossing the wriggling, mewling rabbits
into hessian bags
to be taken home and cut up for Uncle's dogs

his frantic greyhounds
that never did much good
on the racetrack anyway.

Night of Storm

A night of rain
and thunder.
The dog inside
wakes me,
cowering against
the side of my bed.
Trembling dog.
Good dog.
I pat him,
the rain harder now.
No soft toccata this
on the tin and iron roof.
Fully awake now
to the dog's panting,
the black rain
lashing the window,
knife flashes
lustrating
the beating heart.
Black dog.
The room filled
with the smell
of fear.
Boom of thunder,
outside black-robed rain
beating to come in.

The Ache of It

We walked along the beach,
you choosing to talk,
remarking on the persistence
of skilled wind sculpting the waves

and on the dusk,
how it hung over us
like a mosquito net

and then falling
into silence again,
like the shrinking tide.

I wanted to say
I know you ache,
that in time you will heal,
you will shape your life

but too soon the sky
closed around us –
like a fist bruising everything,
like the blackness beneath your eyes.

Variations on Rain in the Time of Drought

1

A trick of light in the kitchen –
a false promise through the pane –
paddocks momentarily are a yellow fluorescence,
thunder and the bounding dog barks
at the menacing sky.

2

Cows coalesce by the dairy,
they lie down in hollows
beneath pockets of bitten trees,
beneath an upside-down sea
of bruised nimbus.

3

Out of the charged sky red with dust
drops ping on the tin and iron roof –
yellow-tailed black cockatoos
rend the sky apart,
they helter-skelter up the dry creek bed
screeching something about rain.

4

In the backlit paddock
dust puffs on the cracked earth of the dam –
on its rim a stray calf's head
is loud with flies…

5

The wind storm passes –
dry leaves and litter
are scattered against the homestead door
like uncollected letters,
like the bills left unopened
on the veranda floor.

Haiku: Loss

Back from the hospice –
on the line his old nightshirt
lifts its empty sleeves.

Cleaning out the drawers –
the scent of his aftershave
on too many things.

These long months after –
for the first time she wakes on
his side of the bed.

Land's Edge, Winter

1

Out on the jetty
the wind pares me to the bone,
the water is pewter and dirty-white-cuffed,
a scrunched grey muslin.

Silver gulls scatter,
tossed into the spray
as if blasted by a giant blow-dryer,
they hold fast, dip and bank sidewards,
clawing the wind's slippery net of sky.

Along the shore plastic bags
are sucked and bloated,
they shoot into air,
chasing the gulls.

Pelicans, hunched into themselves,
clump together beneath the bridge pylons,
boats knock and clang,
slammed against their moorings,
the howling wind gives them no rest

it takes hold of a storefront shutter
and won't let go,
slapping and clunking until it seems
the whole sky will lift off its hinges.

2

Seen from where I stand
in this fading light,
glowering, aubergine clouds
rumble shoreward.

Drops smack like lead ingots
out on the mercuric water,
waves coil and uncoil,
back-slamming the sand.

Like specks of windblown paper
crested terns scatter in the spray,
their querulous cries pitched
across the roiling spume.

Starless and straining,
the sky gives way at its centre,
collapsing on this winter beach
like a black tarpaulin.

Ridge Fire, Morning Alight

The fire seams the horizon
like a brown and yellow scar,
its sparks ignite the haze
the colour of a gas flame flaring,
it reignites the morning's
smouldering cauldron,
setting off an incandescence of leaves,
an awful shrieking of fleeing birds.

Sounds echo like rifle shots
above an endless roaring train
and the reek of cindered heath,
as out of the combustible haze
and down the ridge
this incendiary marches,
incinerating the dull sun and the sky
into a thick black ash.

It sets off spot fires,
torching farm lands,
and leaving in its wake
its ghostly art of charcoal trees,
charred and smouldering carcasses,
and homesteads furnaced to ash
on the valley's floor.

What it is I Wanted to Say

Distracted from writing
I rescue the washing
from the approaching squall.
Drops clatter like flung coins
before the whole sky batters
on the corrugated-iron roof.
It's impossible
to get back to my poem.
I circle the room
and face the window:
it's now a grey blur,
an opaque sheet of running glass.
I take the laundry basket
and place it on the desk.
Slowly, methodically,
the way I had watched you,
I fold the clothes –
the socks, the shirts, the singlets –
arranging them in their piles,
until the rain dies down
and I sit back at my desk,
moving aside the basket
and trying to remember
just what it is
I wanted to say.

Scanning the Horizon

Shoalhaven River, First Light

1

Impatient for the sun's blade
to pare mist from the water
I glance sidewards,
two king parrots spurt past
red and squeaking
and delirious with rain.

2

I slip down out of
the shin-high grasses
to where dark water
languidly slaps
the fishbone sand.
Among the reeds
minnows lip rings on water,
they shatter into bright embers
as the day bursts alive
with wood ducks rising,
their necks and wings
incandescent with fire
raging across the river's skin.

3

On the ridge
I pass from stone to stone,
tapping and splitting,
looking for fossils,
bits of crustacean,
bone shards,
a pine needle.

I bypass crystallised stones,
my eyes seek out others instead:
look, how in this light,
the hair-fine lines
embedded here in a russet vein
resemble a leaf's filigree
or a fingerprint in sand.

I move on,
curious, alone,
hear water relentlessly
churning the banks below me,
whirling mixed pebbles and shells,
erasing history
from the river's floor.

Bagatelles

1

Parrots are colour negatives,
their cries pink

the bleached sky.

Feeding on apples
they are lightly oiled ratchets

contented squeaks
of turning cogs.

2

Raucous cockatoos
wrench the sky apart.

In the tallest limbs
they flower the bare trees white.

3

Magpies tumble
in their net of calls

clinging,
they seem to sing,

'To be heard is enough.'

Coastal Walk

1 Black Swans at the Estuary

The dog startles them,
a convention of black swans
preening and reading the water.

Plashing, they high-step over
the shallow pane of glass,
splintering it into a myriad

sparkling shards,
and as one geometric pattern
flap and lift into air

their loud, rhythmic squeaking
echoing like unoiled winches
over the open plain of water.

2 Jellyfish

After the rain
we carefully step over them,
these extra-terrestrials,
ghostly aliens from the deep,
beached jellyfish
amber as new beer,
crystalline-grey and white dishcloths,
translucent blue lampshades,
umbrellas helpless
as collapsed plastic on the sand,
sticks deliberately thrust through some,
others kicked and flipped over,
gelatinous blobs
drying on the wet strand line,
these off-course invaders,
flying saucers,
discarded spacecraft
from a B-grade sci-fi film.

3 Pipis

On our hands and knees now,
where the hissing ocean
sucks and drags the shore
we watch them bubble and muscle,
arrow and anchor downwards
into the grit and foam, their shells so thin
you'd think they'd be smashed to bits
by the rocks and force of water,
while elsewhere littering the shore
the wide-open ones,
the colour of a bruise inside,
lie unhinged in the sun,
their flesh torn alive by oystercatchers
skittering at the edge of tide.

4 Rock Pool

Late afternoon,
we bend over sheened stones,
whittled and sculpted,
ground down for aeons
upon the sea's lathe,
drawn up and spat out
into this tidal pool,
an underwater intaglio
of polished cobbles –
copper-reds, coal-blacks,
ivory-blues –
a glittering mosaic,
an illuminated storehouse
whose sole window
we look through
is too soon blacked out
by the bruising sky.

T'ai Chi in the Park

Winter Sunday,
in the middle of the city
light chooses white clothing
of the t'ai chi class

their deft heron steps
perfectly articulating presence
as one in exact stance,
as statues slowly awakening

their hands and arms
stretching skywards,
swathing, caressing the air
in balletic grace

drawing down
all the morning's exhaled light,
the sun's impossibly bright streamers
onto the steaming grass.

Mix of Things

Thin veil of mist,
windless dawn.
From the shore's edge before me
a fright of terns
unspools as one shadow
into the paling darkness.
I walk along the wet
estuarine sand
that crescents this coastal village,
its wash of dulling streetlights
seeping down to the water.
My eyes adjust
to the vaporous light,
I see all around me
soldier crabs etching
their secret script,
the rippling surface
where tiny mouths of minnows
lip the liquid sky,
and a white-faced heron
lifting from the shallows
and flying off
into a yellowing gap
in the ragged tea-trees,
the tips of its flapping wings
trailing silver and pearl
over the water.
Already morning
beneath the netted haze
is full with change
and the mix of things.

Eight Haiku

breaking light
the pale vibrato
of cherry blossoms

sudden breeze
every strand of the spider's web
in tune

approaching midday
a lone pine slowly
drinks its shadow

thunder
the scattered pinking
of grass parrots

art gallery
buttoning up my jacket
before a winter canvas

snowmelt
the scent of pine needles
with each step

shadows lengthen
still creaking in the park
the empty swing

night train
the low tones of a stranger's
recent divorce

By the Estuary

1 Morning Comes Alive

Morning comes alive
and with it the crows
flinging their querulous cries
across the brackish water.
A loose-winged heron
rises from the estuary's rim
and lumbers into the acacia and tea-trees;
overhead, a pelican languidly circles,
its wings drubbing the air.
In the grey, estuarine light
I lean into my line,
as if pulled outwards
by the tide now
flipping onto its back
like a caught fish.

2 Weedy Sea Dragon

Walking at low tide,
I step over the sea's cast-offs
and unwanted spillages
of dead and broken things.
Like this weedy sea dragon
caught here in sea wrack
on the drying strand line,
its convex armour
of thorn-like stipples
a subtle speckled-white
and burnt orange,
its underside from its head
to its tail a scimitar
of brilliant yellow pigment.
Sand and rags of weed
cling to its wafer-thin fins
and ribboned appendages.
Where the sun catches
its long, pipe-like
snout and mouth
it takes on an ethereal glow,
its lacquer-black eyes glinting
like china beads,
as if still alive.
Here, along the tideline,
this sea dragon
is more than enough beauty,
more than enough death
for this morning alone.

3 In the Failing Light

Along the shore
fishing boats lie moored
in their afternoon silence

the flushed sky
seeps downwards onto silken water,
tight as the skin of a drum
over the estuary.

Making the most of the failing light,
a flurry of gulls
scatters like flecks of silver

late children shriek and dive
from the pier into the herringed tide,
down into the lathing currents
before scurrying home
with the salt tang still on their skin,
overhead the stark moon
already dreaming.

4 Fruit Bats

At dusk,
after the blistering sun
has burned itself out,
the sky fills
with black clouds,
fruit bats in waves
rising from the island's trees
where all day
they have hung upside down
like black rags.
Wave on wave,
like old black-and-white footage
of wartime bombing raids,
soundlessly their radar
turns everything to black
and the only living things
are the bats overhead
and the raw moon
bleeding over the black inlet

Closing Time

They're moving off: voices and footsteps
scrunching across the pebbled path,
startling an unleashed dog
into a frenetic bark;
shouldering each other
like boats buffeted by wind;
or pedalling off on bicycles so deftly ridden
they barely whisper over the tar.

Even the stragglers in the intimate glow
of the saloon light are jocular,
the shouts square,
the promises of next week's drinks sealed,
the yarns consigned to history,
the publican placing his schooner on the bar.

Returning Home

Evening
is tensed like rusty gauze
between the flushed trunks
of she-oaks.
After a day's work
I am coming home
to the shrill calls of birds
skittering in smudges of dull brush;
grey light lengthening
stencils my shadow
softly on the glass pools.
I walk through
the blady grass
to the door
and turn the knob:
in the perfectly warm dark
of the room
carefully dried birchwood
spits its
welcome.

On Contemplating Morikawa Kyoroku's
Cold Crow, Withered Tree (1680)

Calligraphic
and ink-black,
the crow fills

the gap
in a denuded branch,
spare and flying-white.

Look! it turns away –
What does it see?

Hiking up Bugong Creek

Up Bugong Creek in summer. The air
in the ravine is heavy. You clamber

over mossed stones, fallen logs, leaf litter.
The water tumbles in breathless

children's chatter over rocks and over branches.
After an hour you turn steeply from the creek,

climbing awkwardly through the lantana.
Steeper now, scrambling hand over hand

over rocks. Patches of sky like bright blue cut-outs.
No track through the tangled brush. The skittering wren

flicks its tail like a blue flame before you. This way.
Another turn and over a scree of mottled boulders.

Sweat stings your eyes. The trees thin. Yellow light
scythes through. Standing upright, you look down

to the deep blue sequined water, the steep flank
of eucalypts on the other side, the glinting foil

of a homestead roof on the crest of the ridge.
Late afternoon. You take the fire trail

skirting the ravine. You feast on dried fruit
and drink from your canteen back at the car.

Six Vignettes of the Shoalhaven

1

A skittering tern
oars a smooth parabola
over the skin of water.

2

On dry sand
an old boatshed
leans on its shadow.

3

The keel of a dinghy
a whetted knife
opens a lesion to the sea.

4

Along the shore
a loose balloon
chases the gulls.

5

Wild geese
sweep southwards
an unfurling scarf.

6

Over the estuary
the tap of dusk drips
like an open wound.

Cow Escaped in the Night

Nearing a bend
my headlights pick out
a jigsaw of white
against the moonless black
and veering into a hail of gravel
I come to a shuddering stop
in the mud of the ditch,
steam spewing like white smoke
from beneath the bonnet.

Cursing aloud and shaking,
I think of a night not that long ago
when on this same road
the body of a horse
was launched into the air,
its legs through the windscreen
smashing the driver's skull.

Relieved, I wind down the window
and come face to face
with one crazed eye
of the cow, uncomprehending,
before she swaggers off
trailing her gossamer of spittle
along the roadside fence,
her white now a strange shade of red
in the wash of the ute's tail lights.

The Return

after Dorothy Hewett

This summer I'll go back
past the hedges and strung-wire fences
to that tiny weatherboard house
on the corner of a quiet country street…

I'll walk through the open door
without knocking,
there'll be two boys in shorts
lying on the lounge room floor,
listening to the radio.
They won't see me
as I lean and watch over them
scoring another boundary
in their cricket books.
Their father will be sitting in his singlet,
smoking on the back steps,
with the racing form
and a can of Reschs,
the mother will be in the kitchen
peeling potatoes in the sink
with her little girl
wearing oversized high heels.
It will be hot,
dry air and flies through the screenless windows,
the dog panting in the shade of the Oleander.

Later, I'll watch the boys
hit the ball in the backyard,
the little girl play
with the Irish Setter
while the mother and father
'nip out for a bit'.

The children will be browned
from a summer of swimming at the baths
and running in the open paddocks
behind the house.
One of the boys will leave one day
to work in a bank
and not return,
except for Christmas
and funerals.
The other will finish school
and then leave too.
Only the girl will stay,
marry and raise her family close by.
Falling ill,
the father will never return
from the hospital in the city.
The mother will grieve.
She will grow old,
losing her sight.
The girl will comfort her,
the boys returning
'when they can…'

The weatherboard house will grow quiet.
I'll gently turn back
through the vacant rooms,
disturbing nothing.
I'll find mother napping
in her chair in the sunroom
and not wishing to wake her
I'll leave, quietly latching
the front door shut behind me.

Outside, in the lengthening shadows,
I'll glance back past the hedge
and wire gate
to see her resting still,
her head on her hand,
her body framed in the window,
unmoved, waiting.

From the Headland

after surgery

As if an invisible palm
has drawn aside
a fine lace curtain of rain
sailboarders below me
slice through the chopped swell
clean as flensing blades.

Beneath the bleached-muslin sky
they are deft brushstrokes,
a palette of primaries
cross-hatching and intersecting
on the grey and white
canvas sea.

On the rock ledge
where I sit with my pale legs
thin as oars
dangling in the sheer air
the rain pushes in again,
draping my shoulders,
running its knife-edge of cold
against my skin,
the sails beneath me
already strewn along the dim strandline
like collapsed lungs.

Scanning the Horizon

At six-thirty a.m.
I drive the back road
from Shoalhaven Heads to Berry,
winding past Seven Mile Winery,
the bronze-yellow scarring
the ocean's line of horizon,
past the bed and breakfasts,
round the sweeping bend
of Far Meadow,
avoiding the potholes
that like a cancer refuse to be mended,
watching the bleeding sky behind
turn milk-white ahead,
past Rumbles Earthmoving,
the fiery clusters of the coral trees
lining the road,
to the left, towards Nowra,
orange lights of homesteads
marooned deep in the steaming vale,
the mill smoke drugged and white,
suspended in air,
the near cows like monuments
in the low-level mist
probed here and there
by a scalpel blade of sun,
over Broughton Creek bridge
drowning in its image,
the skin of the water unblemished
but for a solitary duck
cutting a lesion from the farther reeds,

past the Old Creamery
and over the crossing
to the station,
and my three-hour train ride
to where the specialist at her city desk
prescribes for me another, unfamiliar
road I'm now on.

On Finding a Pair of Shoes on the Beach

Like well-worn slippers
placed nightly beside the bed,
these canvas sneakers
with their backs to the sand-dune
face outwards to meet the day.
Why are they waiting here
where there are no swimmers,
the morning being so cold
and the wind whipping
whitecaps off the water?
Is it because their owner,
unable to bring himself
to hurl them over power lines
or dump them in a rubbish bin or skip,
has placed them so lovingly,
so meticulously side by side
out of respect for a lifetime
of faithful service?
I could easily step into them,
being about my size,
but I resist the urge. Instead
I pass quietly by,
leaving them empty like open palms,
or prayer shoes left at the entrance
to a temple.

Postcards from the Coast

1 Winter Beach, Morning

A crescent moon,
the beach and tea-trees
are bleakest at dawn

with crows picking at weed
and sea-wrack
along the steely sand.

Above the thrum
of returning boats
voices toss on the spume

black boardriders,
the first of winter,
slice through the water

and beyond them the sun,
squeezed up from the horizon,
is cut loose
and stains the sea in blood.

2 Estuary at Low Tide

At low tide the wind's finger
crinkles the gulls
volplaning over the estuary –

on the edge of the curving strandline
three fishermen
stand as still as boulders

a lone jogger's shirt
is a tiny stab of red
in the cool opalescence of air.

3 Afternoon, Beneath a Sun-Tight Sky

Startled,
a flurry of terns
unstitches the hem,
trails silver threads
from the estuary's
fine lace-edge.

*

Tattooed in shade
of marram grasses,
a white-faced heron
stands in frozen silence.

*

Darting minnows,
a fistful of pebbles,
stipple the shallows.

*

Along the shore
shadows of the pines
are a thick black calligraphy.

*

Overhead,
a necklace of gulls
rattles the empty bowl of sky.

4 Moon Over the Estuary

After the dusk's slow
inhalation of light

the reticent moon appears
from behind the trees.

Soundlessly, she climbs
the blank staircase of sky

her sequined gown trailing
over the black skin of the estuary.

See how she moves
like mercury through the water

the stars her unstrung pearls
spilling on the floor of the world.

Haiku Sequence: In the Zen Garden

In the Zen Garden
concentric rings of raked sand
dry ocean ripples –

weeping cherry boughs
crepe petals of pink and white
on a dry-stone pond.

In the Zen Garden
cherry petals in the palms
of the stone Buddha –

out of the silence
out of the wood and dry sand
flowering lotus.

In the Zen Garden
this falling cherry petal
this moment passing.

Notes

'Saturdays Home from Boarding School' is after Robert Hayden's 'Those Winter Sundays,' published in *The Anthology of Contemporary American Poetry* Faber and Faber Ltd, 1986.

'Somewhere in Central Australia': during the period 1952–1956, the Australian government allowed British scientists to explode nine atomic bombs in the central Australian desert near Maralinga. In 1986, a Royal Commission set up to investigate the test program concluded that safety standards for the local Aboriginal tribes had been inadequate and that plutonium fragments now poisoned a large area of central Australia.

'Haven': the author gratefully acknowledges Peter Bakowski for lines taken from his poem, 'St Kilda Blues, Melbourne, 1989', published in *Days That We Couldn't Rehearse,* Hale & Iremonger, 2002.

'On Contemplating Morikawa Kyoroku's '*Cold Crow, Withered Tree*': *Cold Crow, Withered Tree* (1680) is one of the Japanese masterpieces from the Idemitsu Collection, which was exhibited in Australia during 1982 and 1983. In Japanese calligraphy, 'flying white' is a brushstroke effect gained by applying pressure to the brush so that the hair separates, leaving streaks of white spaces.

'The Return' owes its inspiration to Dorothy Hewitt's poem 'In Summer', first published in *A Tremendous World in her Head. Selected Poems,* Dangaroo Press, 1989.

Acknowledgements

Acknowledgments are due to the editors of the following publications in which some of these poems, or versions of them, have appeared: *Acorn* (USA), *Akitsu Quarterly* (USA), *Blue Giraffe*, *Chrysanthemum* (Germany), *Divan*, *Eureka Street*, *Famous Reporter*, *fourW*, *Frogpond* (USA), *Ginyu* (Japan), *Going Down Swinging*, *Haiku Presence* (UK), *Hedgerow* (UK), *Island*, *The Mainichi* (Japan), *Notes From the Gean*, *OUTback*, *paper wasp*, *Poetry Canada*, *SALT*, *Shamrock* (Ireland), *The Broadkill Review* (USA), *The Canberra Times*, *The Heron's Nest* (USA), *The Tasmanian Times*, *3Lights Journal* (UK), *Windfall: Australian Haiku* and *Yomimono* (Japan).

Individual poems in this collection have also appeared in *A Lifetime of Words* (Fellowship of Australian Writers, Queensland, 2016 Anthology); Central Coast Poets Inc. Anthology 2006, 2008 and 2010; *Evening Breeze:* Janice M. Bostok Award Anthology 2012; Meuse Press *from the Broken Hill* e-anthology; *Henry Lawson Poetry Anthology* 2008 and 2015; *Idiom 23* (USQ); *Poems in Perspex*: Max Harris Poetry Award 2007; *Poetry & Place* Anthology 2015 (Close-Up Books, 2016); Tarralla 2005 Prize Winning Anthology; and *The Paradise* Anthology 2007.

'This Estuary', 'Ridge Fire' and 'Afternoon, Beneath a Sun-Tight Sky' were three parts of the sequence 'Journey, the South Coast', which was joint winner in the 2017 Venie Holmgren Environmental Poetry Prize.

'Flood-bound: Waiting' was part of 'Drought and Flood', which won first prize in the 2016 Rolf Boldrewood Literary Awards.

Versions of 'Rock Pool' and 'Weedy Sea Dragon' were part of

'Triptych: In the Marine Light', which won first prize in the 2016 Fellowship of Australian Writers North Shore Poetry Competition.

'Land's Edge, Winter' won first prize in the 2015 Fellowship of Australian Writers Queensland Open Poetry Competition.

'Hiking Up Bugong Creek' was part of 'Camping Upriver', which won first prize in the 2015 Henry Lawson Festival Open Poetry Competition.

The haiku 'thunder…' was awarded first place in the 2014 Blue Giraffe Press 2nd Haiku Competition.

'Night Falls' was shortlisted for the 2013 Adrien Abbot Prize.

'Haiku: Loss' was first published in *Australian Love Poems* 2013 (Inkerman & Blunt, 2013).

'Mix of Things' won first prize in the Escape ARTfest 2013 Open Poetry Award and was awarded the Rick and Sarah Stein Award for Literary Excellence.

The haiku 'breaking light…' won an International Sakura Award in the Vancouver Cherry Blossom Festival Haiku Invitational 2013.

A version of 'Variations on Rain in the Time of Drought' won first prize in the Waterline Writing Competition 2011.

'What it is I Wanted to Say' won equal first prize in the Vera Newsom Poetry Prize 2009.

'Small Town, Saturday' was part of the sequence 'Small-town Journal', which was runner-up in the 2009 Banjo Paterson Writing Awards.

Sections of 'By the Estuary' were part of a sequence which won first prize in the 2008 FreeXpresSion Literary Competition.

'Cow Escaped in the Night' was part of a sequence, 'This Land', which won first prize in the 2008 Rolf Boldrewood Literary Awards.

'From the Headland' won first prize in the 2008 FAW Q Inc. Lovers of Good Writing Poetry Competition.

'Saturdays Home from Boarding School' was commended in the 2008 Max Harris Poetry Award.

The haiku 'shadows lengthen…' won third prize in the 2007 International 'Kusamakura' Haiku Competition.

A version of 'The Return' won first prize in the Escape Artfest 2007 Open Poetry Award.

'Along Back Forest Road', 'Small Town, Saturday', 'Bagatelles', 'On Contemplating Morikawa Kyoroku's *Cold Crow, Withered Tree* (1680)' and 'Returning Home' previously appeared in *Conversing With Stones,* Five Islands Press, 1989.

'Somewhere in Central Australia' was previously published in *This Winter Beach,* Seaview Press, 1999.

Versions of 'Coastal Walk', 'From the Estuary' and 'Postcards from the Coast' were part of the Red Room Company's Sea Things project 2009 and broadcast on ABC Radio National's *PoeticA* in 2010.

An unpublished manuscript of *Scanning the Horizon* was runner-up for the Alec Bolton Prize in the 2010 ACT Poetry Prize.

A note on the author

Mark Miller was born in Warren in western New South Wales. He attended school in Orange before graduating with an Honours degree in English Literature at the University of New England in Armidale. His first book of poems, *Conversing With Stones*, won the Anne Elder Award in 1989 and his second, *This Winter Beach*, was published in 1999. He lives on the south coast of New South Wales.

www.ingramcontent.com/pod-product-compliance
Lightning Source LLC
Chambersburg PA
CBHW062149100526
44589CB00014B/1760